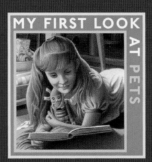

MY FIRST LOOK AT PETS

MANY KINDS OF FISH CAN BE KEPT AS PETS

Fish

VALERIE BODDEN

CREATIVE EDUCATION

Published by Creative Education

P.O. Box 227, Mankato, Minnesota 56002

www.thecreativecompany.us

Creative Education is an imprint of The Creative Company

Design by Rita Marshall

Production by CG Book

Photographs by Corbis (Don Mason), Dreamstime (Aronbrand, Pg Cata, Ecophoto, Sax,

Sergemat, Starper), Getty Images (Mark Horn, Wil Meinderts/Foto Natura, David Nardini,

Chris Newbert)

Copyright © 2009 Creative Education

Printed in the United States of America

Library of Congress Cataloging-in-Publication Data

Bodden, Valerie. Fish / by Valerie Bodden.

p. cm. — (My first look at pets)

Includes index.

ISBN 978-1-58341-722-5

I. Aquarium fishes—Juvenile literature. I. Title.

SF457.25.B63 2009   639.34—dc22   2007051656

First edition 9 8 7 6 5 4 3 2 1

FISH

Smooth Swimmers

Fish can be found all over the world. Some fish swim in lakes. Others swim in the **ocean**. And some live in tanks in people's houses!

Fish have thin bodies. The shape of their body helps fish move through the water. Fish have a tail and **fins**. They use their tail to push through the water. Their fins help them steer and stop.

THE LIONFISH HAS VERY LONG AND FANCY FINS

Fish have eyes on the sides of their head. They have gills, too. Gills help fish breathe. They are right behind a fish's eyes. The gills are covered by pieces of skin that look like half circles.

Fish do not have

eyelids, so they cannot

close their eyes.

A FISH'S ROUND EYES ALWAYS STAY OPEN

Choosing a Fish

There are many kinds of pet fish. They come in all sorts of colors. They come in lots of sizes and shapes, too.

Some fish live in fresh water. Fresh water is water without salt in it. Goldfish live in fresh water that is cool. Guppies live in fresh water that is warm.

Goldfish are not always
orange. They can also be white,
black, or a mix of colors.

Some people like to keep pet fish that live in salt water. Fish that live in salt water are usually colorful. But they can cost a lot of money. This is because they come from the ocean. They can be hard to take care of, too. Clownfish live in salt water.

CLOWNFISH ARE POPULAR PETS IN SALTWATER TANKS

Fish Care

Some small fish can live in a fishbowl. Others need to live in a fish tank. The tank needs to have a **filter** to keep the water clean. It needs an air pump to keep the water fresh. It might need a heater, too. The tank should be cleaned often.

Fish need food every day. Most pet fish eat flakes of fish food. Some like to eat **shrimp** or worms, too.

GOLDFISH CAN LIVE IN A FISHBOWL OR A FISH TANK

Pet fish should not be given too much food. Extra food can make a fish tank dirty. This can make the fish sick. Some fish live only two years. Others can live up to 20 years!

Fish Fun

Fish have to stay in their tanks. They cannot play with their owners like some other pets can. But fish can still be lots of fun.

Snails and some kinds
of fish help keep fish tanks
clean by eating algae *(AL-gee).*

SOME GOLDFISH CAN LIVE FOR 10 OR MORE YEARS

Some fish swim a lot. They can be fun to watch. Other fish like to hide behind rocks or plants in their tank. It can be fun to try to find them.

Some fish can learn tricks. They might learn to swim to their food when they hear a bell. Or they might swim toward the sound of their owner's whistle. And as owners watch their fish swim around and do tricks, they can learn to love them!

MANY FISH LIKE TO HAVE PLANTS TO SWIM BEHIND

Hands-on: Make a Water Filter

Fish need clean water. You can see how a water filter works by making your own.

What You Need

A pitcher of water

A glass

A funnel

Dirt

A piece of paper towel

Sand

Gravel

Cotton balls

What You Do

1. Add a handful of dirt to the pitcher of clean water.
2. Put the piece of paper towel in the funnel. Add layers of sand, gravel, and cotton balls on top of it. These will help trap dirt because dirt is too big to fit through them.
3. Pour your dirty water through the funnel and into the empty glass.
4. Check out your clean water!

PET CATS LIKE WATCHING PET FISH, TOO

Index

Words to Know

algae—plants found in water; algae do not have roots or stems

filter—a machine or object that takes dirt out of water

fins—parts that stick out from a fish's body; fins are usually shaped like triangles

ocean—a huge area of salty water

shrimp—small, thin water animals with 10 legs

Read More

Bozzo, Linda. *My First Fish*. Berkeley Heights, N.J.: Enslow, 2008.

Loves, June. *Fish*. Philadelphia: Chelsea Clubhouse, 2003.

Nelson, Robin. *Pet Fish*. Minneapolis: Lerner, 2003.

Explore the Web

Enchanted Learning: Fish Pages
> http://www.enchantedlearning.com/painting/fish.shtml

FisHedz Aquarium http://www.fishedz.com/index.htm

ASPCA Animaland Pet Care: Fish
> http://www.aspca.org/site/PageServer?pagename=kids_pc_fish_411